Recollections

Part 1

By

Dennis A. Brown

This book is based on a true story; however, some truths may have been amplified for reader enhancement.
"One reader per copy please."

© 2003 by Dennis A. Brown. All rights reserved.

No part of this book may be reproduced, stored in a retrieval system, or transmitted by any means, electronic, mechanical, photocopying, recording, or otherwise, without written permission from the author.

ISBN: 1-4107-0217-0 (E-book)
ISBN: 1-4107-0218-9 (Paperback)

Library of Congress Control Number: 2002096431

This book is printed on acid free paper.

Printed in the United States of America
Bloomington, IN

1st Books - rev. 03/29/03

Table of Contents

"The First Thoughts" 1

"Moving" 6

"Grandma Brown's Funeral" 8

"Time for School" 10

"Mother and Dad's *Different* Relationship" 11

"Mrs. Benton" 12

"Big Snake" 15

"Flogged by a Chicken" 17

"Pickin' Cotton" 19

"Aunt Clara's House" 21

"Learning Personalities"

(Garry & Larry) 22

"Robert" 24

"Ronald" 27

"Dennis" 30

"Debra" 32

"Stringing up Robert" 35

"Robert's Mouse" 37

"Bee Crossing" 41

"Garry's Broken Bones" 43

"Kneel and Pray" 50

"The Sparrow" 51

"My First Whoopin" 52

"Grandpa Jess" 53

"Old Bonco" 58

"Farts" 60

"Getting To Know Myself" 62

"Butch" 66

"Ole Butch and the Preacher" 70

"Easter Chickens" 73

"The Go-Cart" 76

"Goosing" 82

"Escape Route" 84

"Cousin Tom" 86

"Hog Cholera" 91

"Mother's Life Threatening Experience" 96

"Dad and His Ice Cream" 100

"Friends, Family, and Vultures" 102

"Gettin' Speared" 105

"Sandy the Pig" 107

"Peril of the Chickens".......................... 109

"Grandma Shipman" 112

"Grandpa Shipman" 117

"Sonny and Donnie"............................... 122

"The Motorcycle".................................... 125

"The Old Pickup" 133

"King of the Throne"............................... 136

"Morning Games" 138

"The Junk Hole"..................................... 140

"The Auction" 142

"Jackie and Rufus" 144

"The Family Tree" 148

Recollections
"The First Thoughts"

The first thing I can remember in my life, I was about 4 years old, sitting at the kitchen table eating breakfast. I must have had swollen cheeks because I can remember my mother looking across the table and saying, "Dennis looks funny." Then... "My God, Bob! He's got the mumps!" I didn't know what the mumps were, but by the expression on my mom's face, I figured it was deadly! So, I thought to myself, "I guess this is the end to my life already." I went to the living room, knelt on the couch and looked out the window, watching the drizzling

Dennis A. Brown

rain, and waited for the end to come. Of course, it never did.

The year was 1959. I don't know what time of the year it was, but I know there were six of us kids by then. Mother had "had us all in 5 years time," she would later remark. I was too young to really know each of them very well yet, but I was beginning to catch their names. The twins, Garry and Larry, were the oldest, Robert was next, then Ronald, then me, then the last baby...the girl...Debra.

We were sharecroppers on what they called "The Kenny Sister's Farm." We had the outside toilet and a tub on the back porch with a hand pump in the kitchen. There was a trough that

Recollections

went from the pump and through the kitchen window to fill up the tub. There was no hot water heater, so they heated the water up on the stove. We had an upstairs, but the most I remember about the house is the Easter baskets I found on the steps. I learned later that it was one of the nicer houses that we had lived in up to this point. It seems that Dad would farm until he was broke, then go to Michigan to work in the car factories so we could eat. That's why I was born in Flint, Michigan.

The next thing I can remember in my life is moving. I would hear of the great mansion we were moving into by listening to the grown ups. They kept talking about a place where you could go to the bathroom inside the house! I was perplexed by that, wondering how that could be.

I didn't mind leaving the old place, for I was too young to have grown attached to it. But I do remember walking down the gravel road by it, north a little ways, with my brothers to a big ditch where we played. I remember them talking about how our dad had run into it once. Once, we walked to our neighbor's house south of us. They were called the Parrises. We were walking there once and saw a snake, so we ran the rest of the way there and told Mrs. Parris of the "great serpent" we had just

Recollections

encountered. My brother Larry told her that it had spit at us and almost got us!

Dennis A. Brown

"Moving"

Moving day came. Dad was then working for a grocery company called McKnight – Keeton and I guess he had borrowed one of their trucks 'cause that's what we were using to move.

My biggest concern on that day was my tricycle. It seemed like it was never going to get loaded! Trip after trip, it kept being left, but finally, it was loaded and off we went to the new house.... where we could poop inside!

The house wasn't any bigger than the Kenny Sister's place, but I did see the "great

Recollections

ceramic throne" that we were so excited about. What a wonder it was!

The next excitement for me was the concrete sidewalk, which my mom's dad, Grandpa Shipman, prepared for us. It was a miracle for me! At this young age, it had set me free! It was about 30 feet long, and I was out of the house and into the wild open spaces. I could ride back and forth all day long and never get tired.

Dennis A. Brown
"Grandma Brown's Funeral"

Then, the first sad part of my life began. Mother had us all down in the living room and told us that Grandma Brown had passed away. Watching the others, and my instinct, told me I should be sad, but I wasn't and I wondered why. The funeral came and they wanted me to go see Grandma in the room. I didn't want to, but they took me anyway. It was an eerie sight. There she was, high in the air with lights on each side of the casket, with the red shades turned upwards. They called them "blood

Recollections
lamps." I just figured that's where they put her blood.

Dennis A. Brown
"Time for School"

The next thing you know, it's time for school. I must have already been getting pretty witty by then 'cause I remember riding with my mom in the old pickup and saying, "Why do they want me in school? I don't know anything!" That was a big hit with her 'cause she told several other people.

Recollections
"Mother and Dad's *Different* Relationship"

What was becoming evident in my life was that Mother and Dad had a different kind of relationship. It seemed as if they enjoyed fighting with each other. They would argue over almost anything. Mostly they argued over money, it seemed to me, but it could have been anything. I don't remember either one ever being declared the winner. They just fought till they got tired, I reckon. Dad had a voice like a bear and it could shake the windows!

Dennis A. Brown

"Mrs. Benton"

Anyway, I was beginning to enjoy our new place. On the north side was the barn with the regular barnyard animals. We had horses, cows, pigs, dogs, and cats…anything that was needed to survive. Behind the barn, on the north, was a big wooded lot where there were some old junk combines. Later on, we put up a bag swing on an old oak tree where we played a lot. On the south side of the house was a cherry orchard. On the other side of the orchard was the other little house on the place where the Bentons lived. Mrs. Benton was a

Recollections

short woman that seemed to be perfectly round. She seemed nice to me. Roy was her son. He was taller and almost skinny. They had a dog. A little "chi wa wa" that could bark continuously. I always figured Roy lived with his mother because he had "epileptic fits," as they called them. Sometimes he would start hollering and screaming, then finally fall down and pass out. We were taught to act like nothing happened when we saw it happening. Finally he would get up and go about his business. One time he had one when we were chopping cotton. He started screaming and threw his cotton hoe way high into the air and started screaming and wollering around on the ground. Finally, he passed out. He didn't come to until the little "chi wa wa" began licking him on the face. I was again told not to look, so Mother and I chopped on by.

Recollections
"Big Snake"

Anyway, just east of the cherry orchard and the Benton house was kind of a fenced in place that they used to pen up various animals for one reason or another. That's where I had my first close encounter with a big snake. I was sitting on the east side looking west when I caught something out of the corner of my eye. I looked around and there behind me was the biggest brown snake I had ever seen! I was afraid to move. I could swear to this day it was carried on a row of little legs on each side, but I guess that was just my imagination. Anyway,

Dennis A. Brown
I decided to treat it like Roy Benton. I just ignored it until it went away.

Recollections
"Flogged by a Chicken"

There was always something going on with the animals, but you had to learn how to get along with them, learn their ways and not anger or frighten them. I learned this when I tried to pick up a baby chick. It was the last one in a row of baby chicks following their "mother hen." As soon as I tried to pick it up, the mother hen attacked me! I turned and ran for the house as fast as I could with the hen flogging me on the back the whole way! Finally, I made it to the house...hollering and screaming. Mother met me at the door and beat the mad hen off. I didn't mess with any more

chicks.

Recollections
"Pickin' Cotton"

By now, I was just about to mature into "cotton pickin' age." Since I wasn't quite old enough yet, they would have me go on ahead, pick the cotton off the stalk and lay it on the ground in piles. When they got to it, they would just put it into their sacks. Finally, I graduated into a two-bushel bean sack called a "tow sack." It had a rope around the end of it, which would come up under your left arm, around your neck and back down your back to the sack. Best I remember, it held about 30 pounds if it was packed tight. I don't remember

Dennis A. Brown

pulling a "nine footer." I think cotton pickers had come in by then. But, we would still pick the ends off where the picker didn't turn good enough for us. I wasn't much of a picker yet so I still spent a lot of time on the ends with Ronald. We carried water or just played.

Recollections
"Aunt Clara's House"

Once, I remember sitting in the yard at my Aunt Clara's house with a lot of my other aunts. Looking back, it seems most of my aunts were big-breasted ladies. I remember them talking among themselves, teasing me, asking if I wanted a drink of water or anything. I would always decline, and then they would ask me if I wanted some fresh milk and then laugh. I've wondered since then just what kind of milk they were talking about.

Dennis A. Brown
"Learning Personalities"

(Garry and Larry)

By now, I was learning more about my family and each of their personalities, starting with the oldest, Garry. He seemed to take the standard role of second dad since he was older than Larry by twenty minutes or so. Larry always seemed to let him have the role if he wanted it. He didn't care. Larry always said he would have been first anyway, but he had to kick Garry out first. Larry seemed to be content being anywhere or doing anything. He didn't seem to have much preference one-way

Recollections

or the other. However, they were highly competitive with each other, and it never ended. They would slap box each other day in and day out. When they weren't doing that, they were foot racing, rock throwing, walnut fighting, corn cob fighting, or anything they could get their hands on to compete with. To this day, neither would ever succumb to declaring himself defeated. But, I never saw then in a "hating" fight... maybe hurt feelings, but never hating.

Dennis A. Brown

"Robert"

Then, there was Robert. He was a different story altogether. It seemed Robert was born ill and would just not get over it until way up in his older years. I believe he felt he was a little more sophisticated than the rest of us heathens. Picky, finicky, hard to please, whatever you want to call it, he was different. He had his own bed, his own chair at the kitchen table, his own place in the living room, and even his own spot in the car! Wherever we were, he had a special spot and nobody touched it or there were retributions. And he was mean! He even

Recollections

had his own place by the stove so he could be away from us! It was behind the stove. I tried it out when he wasn't around to see what it was like. It didn't seem like a very good spot at all to me! But, it was his spot and he seemed content with it. It was best to let him be than to question his reasons. The rest of us boys just huddled in the front of the stove like "baby pigs competing for the sows tits." Robert's illness could turn into a fight anytime, any place. I guess he fought with all of us except Debra. He wasn't that big or strong or anything, he was just down right mean! If he couldn't beat you with his fists, he would get a club or rock or anything to win. Robert had a hard time, it seemed to me in later years, maturing into a man. I really believed he was destined to probably kill someone and spend the rest of his life in jail. But, by God's grace, he found a good woman and became a state police trooper. I've always heard there is a fine line between cops and criminals. In either case, there needs to be some meanness.

Recollections
"Ronald"

That brings us to Ronald. Good natured, focused, shaky Ronald. He was my sleeping partner upstairs. We got along well together, most of the time. You couldn't hardly make him mad. He would get frustrated "mad" sometimes, but never "mad" mad. He had a black friend down the road that stayed around the house a lot. He accepted everybody pretty well for the way they were. He never thought he was better than anybody else. We had an imaginary line going down the middle of the bed that kept us from fighting most of the time.

But we would erase the line sometimes when it was real cold when we had to huddle to stay warm, cause there was no heat upstairs.

In the summer time, there was a window fan in our end of the room, and we took turns lying by it, sticking our noses to the protective cage to get the full effect of the air movement. The problem was, they got the air on the return side. All we got was the noise. When the window fan was out, we could lie with our heads on the window shelf and look up into the stars. And if you looked long enough, you would almost always see a falling star.

Ronald always had somewhat of the shakes. When he got a little older, I used to watch him

Recollections

glue model airplanes together and wonder how he could do it with the way he shook. But, he always did it. One thing I remember about Ronald, he used to always tell us jokes that didn't seem to be funny, and we would always tease him after he got done with... "Please tell us another joke that isn't funny!"

Dennis A. Brown

"Dennis"

That brings us to me, Dennis. Mother said that my name was supposed to be Johnny, but Bob decided against it at the last moment. I sometimes thought that my name should have been Number 5 because that's what Dad always told people when they asked what my name was. It seems like I was always with Dad. No matter where he was, I was happy to be there, probably because I was fascinated by the farm equipment. I would ride on the combine or tractor or whatever he was on, and never once do I remember getting tired of it or

Recollections

wanting to go home. I always wanted to be the "Indian" of the family. I liked running all day or doing whatever they wanted me to do. Being small for my age for most of my youth, I was the family "gopher". Anytime they needed someone small to dive in and get anything, they would call on me. I was happy to contribute. I really did feel that Garry was my second dad. He always picked me in basketball or in anything we all did, even though he knew I wasn't that good. Anyway, that's about the way I saw myself, and since I'm writing this story, that's the way it was.

Dennis A. Brown

"Debra"

Last, but not least, there was Debra, "the only girl." Mother began to cry when the doctor told her she was pregnant again. She already had five boys in four years and didn't know if she could bear having another. There was no way of knowing back then what the baby might be. It could be another boy or... a girl! They were on hard times back in Michigan, trying to make up for more farm losses. Seeing Mother cry and having pity, the doctor mentioned abortion. Well, this was highly immoral back then and Mother said,

Recollections

"No." The doctor then said that there were measures she could take herself that might lead to a miscarriage. That was okay to try. She worked hard, ran up and down the steps, and did whatever she could to encourage a miscarriage. But, luckily, nothing worked. She was healthy as a horse and nothing was going to stop this baby. Thus, Debra made it. Debra had a special room by herself downstairs off from the kitchen. I wasn't jealous, but she had heat down there! I always felt kind of sorry for her when she had to bear the brunt of some of Mother and Dad's fights. Another thing I remember about Debra is that one Christmas, we must have had another bad year because all she got was one of the ugliest dolls I have ever seen in my life! So, there you have it. Six kids in five years and we were close.

Recollections
"Stringing up Robert"

Then, there comes to mind when Garry and Larry had been watching too much "Gun Smoke." They had seen many hangings there and decided it was time to string somebody up. No one knows how, but they had somehow coaxed Robert into being the one to get hung. I guess Robert thought he was going to be the star of the show. He obligingly got in the little red wagon and put the rope they had tied to the close line around his neck. After telling him of all he had done wrong, one of them pulled the wagon out from under him. Needless to say, it put a tremendous strain on Robert's neck. He couldn't breath, and had done run out of tippy toes before he could get the pressure off. Garry and Larry just stared at him wondering what the problem was. Luckily, Grandma Shipman happened to be looking out the back window when it happened. She was a big woman and when she came through the back porch door, she damn near tore the hinges off! She ran to the clothesline and got the poor boy down. The rest of us scattered like a covey of quail. Maybe that's why Robert was always so ill.

Recollections
"Robert's Mouse"

Still another episode of Robert comes to my mind. Dad, Garry, Larry and Robert were chopping cotton on Uncle Lloyd's farm just south of Dudley. Ronald and I had been left on the end in the peach orchard when all of a sudden, I heard the most hair-curling scream of my life! I looked up and it was Robert. He was swirling around in the dirt like a tornado and Dad was running toward him. All the while, I'm thinking, "Well, that's it. Robert's gone too far now and Dad's going to tear him up." And sure enough, Dad was jerking his pants down to what I thought was the set up for the whooping of his life! What had actually happened was that a mouse had done run up Robert's leg and was circling in his underwear like it was in the Indy 500! They said Robert was hollering, "Help me, Daddy! It's got a thousand legs!" Finally, they got the mouse out, and after a brief rest, it was back to chopping cotton. But, I bet Robert kept his eye out for mice for the rest of the day.

When I was finally and regrettably old enough to chop cotton and chop out more weeds than cotton, I was put to work. There cannot be a more mind-dulling, unrewarding job than chopping cotton. You never wanted to

Recollections

look down the row or across the field because it never ended. The only reward was when the sun was going down, you got to quit. The only thing that might speed you up is that if you got to the end first, you generally got to pick your next row. But, usually, when you picked one that looked like it might be easy, you would later find out, like the country western songs would later say, "You had done picked another hard row to hoe." The only thing you really wanted to look at was the clouds, 'cause if it rained, you got to quit. It was also a little exciting because it was dangerous. Many people had been killed when the cotton hoe, "being an excellent ground," would attract the lightening and kill the operator. To some, that might not have been so bad.

Recollections
"Bee Crossing"

There was an eerie time when I was chopping cotton with only my brothers on the old home place southwest of Frisco. First, I heard this eerie, dull, high-pitched sound. Then, the sun was beginning to shade out. I didn't know what was happening. But, I have always been impressed with my brother's good sense. I didn't know which one it was, but I always reckoned it was Larry who started a low-pitched holler with a commanding, "GET DOWN, GET DOWN!" Still not understanding what was the matter, I followed the command and got down. When I realized what it was, a cold chill ran down my back. A large hive of bees was on the move! They were migrating directly over us! Hundreds of thousands of them! We lay there between the rows for what seemed like forever until they finally passed. My fear was compounded in later years when I found out the dangerous peril we were really in.

Recollections
"Garry's Broken Bones"

I guess if there had been a record kept, it would show that Garry had broken more bones in his body than the rest of us put together. I think it started out with a bicycle race after school after a baseball game. Garry and some other boys were racing. Nothing wrong with a bicycle race, except they were racing to the brick wall of the gymnasium and "sliding" to a stop. You guessed it. Garry's chain came off and he couldn't "slide" to stop. So, he went head first over the handlebars and into the brick wall. The only thing he had to stop himself with were his arms. You guessed it again, yep, both of them, broke clean as a whistle. Snapped like dry sticks. Compound fractures, they called it. So, there he was, thirteen years old with two broken arms. These were the formative years and he couldn't even pee without help. He couldn't scratch, eat, turn a book page, and God knows...he couldn't wipe his own butt. So, guess who those jobs went to.... yep, Larry. And, in retrospect, Garry was lucky to have a twin brother in this situation. He still had to go to school and Larry had to help with all the "natural" duties. It all had to be frustrating for Garry. When he took his baths, they had to take a leaf out of the kitchen table and lay it across the tub so he could lay his casts on it. He was always an active kid, and when the frustration peaked, I remember that all he could do was jump up and down while holding his casts level. But, the casts finally did come off, and he was back to slap boxing with Larry.

The next thing to break on Garry was his foot. I don't know if it was all his fault or not this time, but he had his foot in the wrong place at the wrong time. Dad, Garry and Larry were back on the back forty, on a 30 Ferguson tractor plowing with a two bottom-breaking plow, back by a place which was always called Pig Turd Island. Don't really know why they called it that, but that was what its name was. It was just a little island where the slough went on both sides of it. Anyway, Garry and Larry were riding on the fenders of the tractor, and Garry must have left his foot on the axle and when Dad let the plow down, the arms went down on his foot and crushed it. To make it a thousand times worse, the tractor died in this position and would not restart. Then, Dad decided to run to the house to get a truck or something to help get the thing started, an idea Larry wasn't too keen on because he really didn't want to hear the painful moaning. So, Dad starts out running from the farthest place on the farm. Ronald and I were at the house

Recollections

playing by the chicken house when I heard someone hollering. I looked up the field road and there was Dad. His run had done turned into a walk and he was hollering something. He just kept on hollering. Didn't now what was wrong, but I knew it must be bad. I ran to the house and Mother was there talking to someone who was just leaving. I said, "Dad's coming up the field road and he's mad or something." She didn't act as concerned as I thought she should, but she got into the car and headed toward Dad. When she got to him, he jumped in the driver's side and tore up the field road in that 1959 Pontiac station wagon. In the meantime, Larry had somehow gotten the old tractor started and got it off Garry's foot. Next thing I know, I'm on the front porch, Dad pulls up from the field road, lets Larry out, and completely tears up the gravel road in front of our house as he is leaving. I don't know why, but the excitement of Dad leaving like that made me laugh. Larry looked at me tersely and said, "I don't think it's very funny." I didn't either, but I couldn't explain my laughter, so I just quieted down.

Garry broke various different bones in his body quite frequently. But the last prevalent one I remember was his hand. He and Robert had gotten into it one night, and since Robert probably didn't figure he could whoop Garry in hand-to-hand combat, he found a club and beat him with it. Larry came to the rescue and broke them up. They decided not to tell Mother and Dad what really happened and made up a story. But, what I remember most vividly is that the doctor set Garry's hand with no anesthesia. Mother never liked that doctor from then on.

Dennis A. Brown
"Kneel and Pray"

When I was young, I always felt like I was put here for some reason. I didn't know what the reason was, but I always felt I was here for a purpose. Sometimes this feeling would overwhelm me, and I remember I would go out to the back yard and kneel down and pray. Didn't really know what I was really praying for, but I would kneel and pray. Somehow, it made me feel better.

Recollections

"The Sparrow"

One day I came out of the back porch and there was a sparrow that had landed on a limb. I don't know what happened between me and the sparrow, but I knew it wasn't afraid of me. I walked over to it and petted it on its head and it just sat there. I backed up and watched it for a moment and it just flew away. I really don't know what it all meant.

Dennis A. Brown
"My First Whoopin"

In my youth, I can remember the only time my dad ever whooped me. Dad, Mother and I were the only ones home and they wanted to take a nap and I wanted someone to talk to. I knew they were taking a nap, but I kept on riding my bike on the porch and making noise. Finally, Dad had enough and came out and whooped me with a belt. The belt didn't hurt that much, but my feelings were pretty crushed. I sat out front under the old mimosa tree and cried. Later, Dad came out and told me he was sorry. I felt better.

Recollections
"Grandpa Jess"

There was no man I admired more than my dad, unless it would be Grandpa Brown, Jess. With people, there is a bond of personalities that knows no age difference. Grandpa and I were bonded. We were one and the same. Not till long after he was gone did I understand this bond. He never said it, but in my heart, I felt that I was his favorite. He used to wrestle me down and chew on my ear. It was the weirdest thing I had ever felt, but it made me laugh. He kept me from ever chewing tobacco because he would always take out his Bull of the Woods chewing tobacco and try to make me take a chew. It smelt bad. When my baby teeth were coming out, he was the only one I would let pull them. I would always wait for him to come over, and he would take his wire pliers and pull them out. It never did hurt.

One of the most prevalent things I remember about Grandpa Brown was one time we were dynamiting stumps out by the cherry orchard. He had dug under the stump and placed the dynamite, put the caps into it, and run the fuse out about three feet. Then, he lit the fuse. My brothers and I were behind a log about 200 feet away. Grandpa jogged back to the log and waited for the charge to go off.

Recollections

But, it didn't. We waited for a long time and Grandpa got impatient and said, "I better go check it." He had no more than stood up when the charge went off. It was the funniest thing to me. The charge went off brilliantly and the stump went at least 150 feet into the air. With roots going everywhere, he hollered, "GET DOWN, BOYS!" He fell to his knees, bent over and covered his head. I was more interested in where those roots were going to land, so I stayed up and kept my eyes on them.

Grandpa was an honest man, and you could tell that people trusted and respected him. He once lost two of his fingers in a corn picker. He was on the back forty and had to drive his car to the house. He said later that he couldn't hardly see to drive because the blood kept squirting out of his hand and onto the windshield. They said that when he was recuperating at the house, he would sometimes rise up, look into the dresser mirror and ask, "Who's that old man?"

One of the things I regret most in life is the one time Grandpa came down to the old home place where we were living. We were eating breakfast, and he said he couldn't sleep the night before. He kept thinking about me and him going back to Old Shawnee Town, Illinois, and seeing the place where he grew up. I know he wanted me to take him. I was about sixteen

Recollections

at the time, but I had a girlfriend and I wouldn't leave. He wouldn't ask me straight out because he was a proud and unselfish man. God knows that I have regretted not taking him ever since. They called him Mr. Brown.

Dennis A. Brown
"Old Bonco"

Going on to more humorous recollections, Dad bought us a riding horse one time and we named him Bonco. He was a black and white, medium sized horse. And he was "meaner than hell!" He was supposed to be a family pet, but was far from it. Bonco was impossible to ride because he would bite and buck off anyone who tried to ride him. Finally one day, Dad decided to "break" him. He got on him and rode him as hard as he could. Dad thought he had good control of him when all of a sudden Bonco ran as hard as he could to a road ditch,

Recollections

planted his front feet and threw Dad over his head and into a ditch. Dad was madder than hell and came up and hit Bonco in the face with his fist. But he never rode him again. We were all scared to ride him after that. But Garry and Larry had learned how to have good sport with him. They had just acquired some new BB guns, and they found out that every time they would shoot Bonco in the butt, he would buck and fart! They used to have friends over to watch this rare phenomenon and Bonco would never let them down.

Dennis A. Brown

"Farts"

...And speaking of farts, my brother Ronald had somehow become a connoisseur and expert in the art of farts. He is the only person I know of that had the ability and talent to palm a fart. He could fart, catch it in his hand, run up to 100 feet, throw it in your face and it would still be good. I acquired some talent in the art to where I at least had the ability to contend with him. 'Cause if I hadn't, he would palm one while we were in bed and put it under my pillow. With some of the palmed fart talent, he

Recollections

knew that I could somewhat retaliate and this bit of knowledge held him in check.

Ronald truly enjoyed his farting talent. He soon learned that he could also fart in a fruit jar, seal it up and it would keep good for weeks. He never ran out of ammunition. And he was always good about sharing his talent with anyone that cared to listen.

Dennis A. Brown
"Getting To Know Myself"

About this time in life, I was beginning to learn a little about my physical anatomy through listening to my older brothers and their friends, and a little personal experimentation. I acquired the art of what they called Jack-n-off. There was a special thing on my body, safe between my legs, that everybody called a wee-nee. I had one and all my brothers and our friends had one. The "boys" had one, that is. At this point in time, there really wasn't much interest in girls. Anyway, when you rubbed on the wee-nee just right, it would stiffen up and

Recollections

stay stiff. It felt pretty good. And if you stayed with it long enough, it would finally start thumping, feel even better, then fall over dead. Although everyone talked about it, it was more of a personal game that you wanted to play by yourself unless a bunch of guys got together and had a race to see who would get done first. I had a friend later in life who always claimed in one of the races, he came in both first and third place. But nobody ever believed him.

It was a game that everybody knew about, but you didn't want to get caught at it. For some reason, it seemed all right if you announced to everyone what you were fixin' to do, but if you got caught at it, they would laugh and tell everybody. I have seen friends almost ruined for life after getting caught. You had to be pretty close to someone before you wanted to talk about it, although it was generally assumed everyone knew of the art. But you knew there was something not quite right about it. That was the part of the body that your parents never talked about. But I guess it seemed like an innocent sin to us. We just kept on experimenting.

Once a cousin of ours came to stay with us for a night or two. He was about Ronald's and my age so he was placed in the bed right between us. Sometime in the night, I guess he decided he needed to jack-off. He didn't bother

Recollections

to discuss his intentions with Ronald or me. He just started in. We just ignored it and played like we were asleep. It was one of the most disgusting things we had ever experienced. He worked on it so hard that I thought he was going to bounce clean out of the bed! It was the most flagrant abuse of the art we had ever witnessed. His reputation in that respect was ruined for us for the rest of time. And we still talk about it to this very day.

Dennis A. Brown

"Butch"

And that brings us to ole Butch. Ole Butch was a mixed breed dog that mostly resembled a mix between a rabbit dog and a hound dog of some sort. He wasn't pretty or ugly, he was just Butch, certainly not an intelligent dog but not much trouble. Ronald brought him home one day without even asking anyone. He had gotten him from a friend named Dennis Joseph. Everyone looked at him and generally agreed that he wasn't much of an asset to the farm. But Ronald was adamant about keeping him so Dad let him stay. We already had a

Recollections

small collie dog named Snoopy that was smart. Snoopy was generally known as Debra's dog because she used to talk to it in dog language. She would actually bark to it and the dog would mimic the sound and bark back. I don't know if they were actually communicating, but it would go on for quite some time.

Anyway, Butch seemed to fall into the tribe okay. He didn't give much trouble. He was a mild mannered dog, and one day some of us boys were standing around talking about jack-n-off. Since there wasn't much to do for excitement around the old farm, we wondered if ole Butch might like a stroke or two. Don't know who was really first, but somebody was

Dennis A. Brown

talked into it. And low and behold, Butch liked it! But it was plain to see you couldn't help him much because his legs would get to rotating right off like he was running in the air and they would scratch your arm all up. But it seemed that he did appreciate the attempt. After that, Butch got to where he would sometimes run up to one of us boys and roll over on his back in anticipation of a stroke or two. If we had time and no one was around, we would try to oblige him. Sometimes we would show our friends how we had trained him, and they thought it was funny too. Dad never caught on to what we were up to, but he did wonder why Butch would sometimes run up to people and roll over on his back. He would sometimes say, "I wonder what in the hell is wrong with that dog?" We kept our silence and just looked at each other.

Dennis A. Brown
"Ole Butch and the Preacher"

One day, one of the funniest things we had ever seen happened. Dad had invited the preacher over for supper. He was one of the nicest people I had ever met and everybody in the community liked him. He didn't have anything and didn't really want for anything. He truly was just into the soul saving business.

Anyway, it was just before suppertime. Some of the boys were in the front yard and Dad and the preacher were swaying on the front porch swing. Butch rounded the corner of the house and his eyes locked in on the preacher's leg. He had on a pair of bright colored, double-knit, checkered pants. Butch fell immediately into a deep and lustful love. He ran up to the preacher, locked on and went to work. We were aghast at what we were witnessing. Butch had never done anything like that before and would never do it again. But, there was no stopping him. He was possessed. The preacher tried to ignore it for a second, then began to try to shake him off. But, Butch was locked on like a cocklebur on a shoestring! The preacher couldn't shake him. After the embarrassing episode went on for a while, Dad also joined in the fight to save the preacher's leg. We boys just stood there bug-eyed, watching the nightmare before our eyes. Butch would not relent from his hold. Finally, Dad went to kicking Butch. Each lick was harder than the last. Finally, Dad gave up trying to reason with him. He reared back and plowed his work boot right into ole Butch's rib cage as hard as he could. Apparently the pain had overcome Butch's obsessive passion and he cut loose. Running down the porch with Dad hot on his trail, Dad chased him clean around the house. Dad came back around the corner of the house, acting like nothing much had happened and said, "Well, let's go eat." So we did.

Recollections
"Easter Chickens"

The next thing to show up on the farm was the Easter chickens. Back then, at Easter time, you could go to the store and buy colored baby chickens. What they would do is insert a dye into the egg before the chicken would hatch. It would come out colored in almost any color you wanted. This particular year, someone had bought two for us. One was blue and one was yellow. We kept them on the back porch for a long time when they were young. We kept them in a cut off piece of linoleum that was about six inches tall and curled around in a circle like a spin wheel. They could walk around but couldn't get out. Anyway, when they got older, we had to get them out of the house. We watched them pretty close, but somehow, the dogs ate the blue one. As an attempt to save the yellow one, we would take it outside, put it by the dogs and when they tried to get it, we would beat the heck out of them. After several lessons, they learned not to mess with that particular chicken. From then on, when they even got close to it, we would kick them. Somehow, the Easter chicken became aware of this and would actually taunt the dogs by running up to them, spread its wings and scare the dogs. The dogs had learned that if the Easter chicken got close, they got beat. They were pretty scared of that.

For a good while, the Easter chicken ruled the barnyard. One day, a strange dog happened to come down the road. The Easter chicken ran out to greet the pesky dog and spread its wings. The stranger didn't run. The chicken didn't realize that its power was restricted to the yard, and the strange dog had not yet been "properly" introduced to the Easter chicken. Therefore, the dog ate the Easter chicken on the spot. There was nothing left but feathers. That was the end of the Easter chicken.

Dennis A. Brown
"The Go-Cart"

Somewhere in this story, Ronald and I had located a go-cart that we wanted to buy. It was a farmer's son's that lived north of us about ½ of a mile. He wanted $40 for it. Seemed like a high price back then, but we didn't figure he would come down on the price because by "our standards," they were rich. We knew this for sure because one 4th of July, we were setting off firecrackers. There were five or six of us setting off our usual "one firecracker at a time." When we set ours off, we thought they could hear us and were answering with a volley of their own. But their volley was always bigger and longer. We wondered just how many people were up there. We later found out that they were actually setting off whole packages of firecrackers! We decided that they must be rich.

Anyway, Ronald and I decided that no matter what, we were going to get that go-cart. It took a whole summer of chopping weeds out of the beans and cotton, but finally at last, we had saved enough money to buy it. Somehow, Mother had discovered that we had the money and began to pressure Dad to relieve us from it. But, this was one time Dad was going to stick to his guns and allow the deal to go through. I did feel bad about it because I knew they really needed the money. But anyway, we paid the $40 and the go-cart was ours! The only trouble was that the drive chain wouldn't stay on. It fell off continuously. Dad couldn't take the time to look at it, and we definitely didn't know how to fix it. The only way we could make it stay on is if we only circled to the left. So we finally accepted that it was a left-handed go-cart. So, everywhere we went, we had to be going to the left. It was really a highway go-cart with small solid wheels, and not really suitable at all for gravel roads or yards. It was set real low to the ground and was on a solid frame. There was nothing to absorb the shock.

Recollections

Our skinny little butts absorbed the shock. The bounce came through the hard wheels, through the frame, up our bodies, to our head and shook our eyeballs. I mean to tell you that when you were riding it, you couldn't see anything but a blur. But that didn't stop us. We simply got our older brother's Boy Scout belt, wrapped it around the frame and around our waist and held on. You still couldn't see anything, but you weren't afraid of being thrown out. As long as you circled the house to the left, you could run.

We both enjoyed our new go-cart, but a partnership is a hard thing to deal with. It was such an addictive vehicle. So we decided to take three laps around the house and swap off. This worked fairly well until the count got off. I was on the cart on what I had counted as two laps. I guess he had counted three. I kept going. Ronald was hot on my trail and chased me all the way around the house. To the left, of course. Catching me, he told me how I had cheated him and he wasn't going to stand for it. I told him, "I'll go another round if

I want to!" When I tried to take off, that's when he pulled the spark plug wire and set the engine on fire with all the gas that had vibrated out! Then, Ronald just stood back and stared at the burning go-cart with his eyes all bugged out. I couldn't get the damn Boy Scout belt to

Recollections

undo! Excited as I was and try as I might, it wouldn't release. I hollered for help and Ronald took another step backwards. It really looked like it was going to blow for sure! Finally I got loose and started running through the back door and out the front hollering over and over, "THE GO CART'S ON FIRE! THE GO CART'S ON FIRE!" I kept on running around the house until somebody caught me and told me that Dad had put the fire out with a tow sack. I was a little embarrassed, but regained my composure and went back to fight with Ronald. It wasn't long before the go-cart quit running. We didn't have the money to fix it anyway.

Dennis A. Brown

"Goosing"

Another thing that was big around the house was a deal called goosing. It wasn't a game, it was just a hazard you lived with considering there were five boys so close together. We were most all the time, especially at night, running around in our underwear. This was excellent for a good hunt of goosing. What you didn't want to do in those circumstances was bend over around any of the boys or they would try to poke a finger in your rear end. If they succeeded, it was call "a goose." This was one of the most horrible things you had ever felt, especially if you had loose underwear on. Goosing could be as dangerous for the gooser as for the goosee! When the goosee got his breath back, he was looking to kill somebody! And, for the first 100 feet, he probably would have. But, after that far, you would usually calm down to just wanting to whoop somebody if you could. For the gooser, the trick to getting away with it was to be ready to run as soon as you had landed a good hit. You didn't quit running and you never looked back. The key was to stay away from your victim for at least an hour.

Dennis A. Brown
"Escape Route"

If you ever needed a fast escape from anything, there was always the TV antenna. It was on Garry, Larry and Robert's side of the room. It came up from the ground all the way above the roof. There were many a time we had sneaked out down the ole TV antenna like a bunch of firemen. But you needed to be careful of where you landed because it was on the "peeing window" side. You couldn't pee out the side that Ronald and I were on because of the window fan. It was a lot easier to pee out the window than to go downstairs and wait for

Recollections

the bathroom to get free. The main problem was that when the screen was in and you peed through it, it would stink up the room. They would make you stop and go pee downstairs until the mosquitoes were gone and they took the screen down.

Dennis A. Brown
"Cousin Tom"

Cousin Tom was about my age and seemed almost like the sixth brother to me. We were together almost as much as Ronald and I were. If he wasn't at my house, I was over at his house. Tom and his family were a really neat family. I reckon you had to be if you were going to live in the city. Tom always helped wash dishes, sweep floors and always made his bed in the mornings. We, on the other hand, weren't quite like that. Mother had already given up a few years earlier. Trying to control five wild Indians in basically a one room

Recollections

upstairs proved to be too much for her. She surrendered, coming up only if the fights got so intense that she thought someone was badly hurt.

Tom still talks about one of the times he stayed with us. When seeing clothes and blankets scattered everywhere, he asked, "Where do I sleep?" We looked at him oddly and said, "Just grab some covers and lay down!" I guess he soon got used to it.

Tom lived on the poor side of town called the "Cotton Belt." I don't know why they called it that! He liked it in the country with my brothers and the farm animals. I liked it in the city where the streets were paved and you could ride your bike. Tom was my wrestling partner. We wrestled continuously, seldom getting angry at each other. His mom was a real nice lady. I remember her sitting me on her lap and hugging me. That was something that didn't happen much around my house. Guess there wasn't much time for that. She was special to me. His family and my family were constantly going camping together. The fun we had would take too many pages to write about.

But, suddenly a lot of the fun stopped. Something that rarely happened or rarely was even spoken of back then happened. Tom's mom and dad got a divorce.

Recollections

The grown-ups talked about it like it was the plague. They whispered around, but you could figure out what they were talking about. Things changed, and people acted really different. All of a sudden, and they moved into a new house uptown. But it didn't seem so nice with so much unhappiness around. I didn't stay with Tom as much as I once had. But I do remember one particular night that I stayed. We had just gone to bed in a room in their basement. We had been lying there quietly when out of the silence came Tom's voice. "Everyone done all they could, you know." Those words still echo in my brain like words on a tombstone. I lay there in the silence, knowing he wished we could talk. I searched for words but none would come out. We fell asleep.

Recollections
"Hog Cholera"

It seemed like there were always animals dying for one reason or another. And when they died, they had to be burnt as quickly as possible. This kept diseases from spreading. It was always sad to see the animals die back then, partly because you missed them, mostly because of the money. We had one ole bull that I believed Dad wished would have died. He didn't have a name, we just called him "Ole' Bull." He was meaner than hell! He hated everyone and would never stay penned up. Every time he got out, Dad would have to hunt him down and herd him back home. Dad didn't have time for that. He herded him back for the last time one day. Ole' Bull had gotten out and Dad went after him with the tractor. He somehow must have lassoed the bull because when he came back with him, he was tied to the tractor. The problem was the bull had planted his feet in an attempt to stop the tractor but the little tractor had won. It was draggin' Ole' Bull down the gravel road on his side! I still remember Ole' Bull's face. His eyes were crossed and his tongue was hanging out. Dad was looking straight ahead. The bull was sold soon after.

Recollections

A cow we did have to burn is one we hated to lose. It seems that there was a load of soybeans on a flatbed trailer inside the barn and somehow, this cow had gotten into it. And that spells trouble for a cow. Cows don't really know when to quit eating. Worse yet, you never feed them soybeans because the soybeans swell about five times their normal size after they have been digested. That's another odd thing I remember seeing. After finding that cow the next day, it had swollen five times its normal size. It was an odd looking thing with its legs straight out and almost straight up into the air. Its skin was stretched to the max and I was afraid it was about to pop if I touched it. So I stood back.

Dad's next big money making scheme was to get into the hog business in a big way. We wound up with a whole lot of powdered milk from an ex-sheriff friend of his named Jim. I believe the sheriff got it off a wrecked train and sold it to Dad cheap. Dad thought he had done figured a way to turn that cheap powdered milk into the profitable meat of a pig. I remember us kids pouring the powdered milk into the hog troughs and mixing it with water. We would stir it with a stick 'till it looked like real milk and the hogs would drink it up! But then the powder must have gotten wet because the bags started to turn into big hard chunks that you had to break up with a hammer. The chunks would just float in the water. The pigs would have to catch the chunks with their mouths as they floated in the water.

It wasn't long after that, till the pigs started getting sick. They had what they called Hog Cholera. Dad decided he had better take the healthy ones off before they got sick too. But it was too late. They were all infected and they all died. We had thirty pigs that Dad had bought with borrowed money and thirty hogs died. There was no relief from the money plights or fights.

Dennis A. Brown
"Mother's Life Threatening Experience"

One day we were having just a regular everyday normal evening. Mother had gone outside earlier, I reckoned just to get away from it all for a while. I was coming from the living room into the kitchen when mother staggered in the back door. She was crying uncontrollably holding her head, and her hair was completely messed up like she had just walked out of a tornado. Dad was already standing in the kitchen, and immediately upon seeing mother's condition, rushed outside to deal with the perpetrator. Exiting the back

Recollections

door, he ran to each corner of the house to see which way they had run. However, there was nothing. He came back into the house where we were watching mother with fearful awe. She was sitting at the kitchen table still sobbing when she began to reveal and unravel the horrible episode. We listened with horrid anxiety. As I had expected, she said she had gone out just to get away from it all. Spying a lawn chair we had just acquired, she moved toward it. It was one of those flat lawn chairs that lay out completely flat without armrests. Mother, apparently not being accustomed to the mechanics of the device, attempted to sit down and relax in it. That's when the true nature of the killer lawn chair revealed itself. She plopped her rear in the center of the thing and the end of it came up and whacked her on the back of her head. She lunged forward from the pain of the blow, and the legs from that end folded down, and the other end came down and whacked her on the forehead. Knowing she was losing the fight, she attempted to escape. That's when the last legs fell, and both ends hit her again simultaneously. She knew then that she would have to make a desperate attempt just to save her own life. With her remaining strength she tried to lurch away, but the lawn chair wasn't through yet. It had completed its fold and grabbed her by the ankle, and she dragged it another ten feet before it would release its hold. While we were trying hard to keep from laughing, Dad went out to make sure the life was gone from it, and the place was safe again.

Dennis A. Brown
"Dad and His Ice Cream"

One good thing about Dad is that he loved ice cream. He didn't drink beer or anything like that, but he did have a weakness for ice cream. He didn't mind spending money for it, if we had the extra. And it was good for us too! The ice cream man used to deliver out to the farm because dad would almost always get a couple of gallons if he had a little extra money on him.

Dad pretty well always took things in stride. I remember one time we had the prettiest corn crop I thought we'd ever had in a field right beside our house. Then all of a sudden, a big storm came up and hailed on the corn. We were all watching it from the cellar window. We watched it go from knee high corn to just green stubs sticking out of the ground. As young as I was, I knew it was bad and I felt sick inside. I was wondering what Dad's reaction was going to be. When he came out of the cellar, he looked around and said, "Wasn't that a hell of a storm? Ya'll want some ice cream?" I guess he figured what was done was done and there wasn't much he could do about it now. But, it meant even more hard times on down the road.

Dennis A. Brown
"Friends, Family, and Vultures"

It looked like we were on our last leg. Dad was down to less than 120 acres. He was even talking about selling the combine and having the crop threshed, a thought that made me sick inside. Without a combine, I thought we were dead for sure.

It's funny when you're down and out that others can "smell a kill." We had a neighbor who was "financially" well respected around the neighborhood and he kept stopping by. The worse we looked, the more he would stop. One day while Dad and I were on the porch swing, he stopped by and made small talk for a good while, then left. Upon the neighbor's leaving, Dad said, "Ole, so-n-so thinks were done for." That's all he said.

But lo and behold, about this time we had an uncle in California who worked for the postal service. He had enough money and wanted to buy a farm for Dad to rent! It wasn't much land, but it was enough to hold us together.

And there was more help. Hubert and Mildred Swinger were just one mile east of us and somehow, they saw our plight. There were no better people to me than Hubert and

Dennis A. Brown

Mildred Swinger. They practically lifted us up from what was in my mind poverty.

When we chopped cotton for them, they paid more than anybody. When Dad threshed beans or corn for them, they paid more than the average custom rate. My respect for them was and still is greater than any other person I have met. You had to work hard, but you were paid good. I started smoking when I was young, and they were the only people I ever refused to smoke in front of, out of respect. I wanted to show them a person better than he really was, I guess.

Recollections
"Gettin' Speared"

Then times started getting a little better and the ice cream started flowing in again. Once after supper, I had just fixed me a bowl of ice cream and was eating it while I walked out to the front porch. It had crossed my mind about where Ronald had gone to so fast, until I stepped off the porch. I took about three steps on the sidewalk when I heard an Indian scream from above. When I looked up, Ronald was up in the old cedar tree and the cane pole spear he had was already released from his grip. You guessed it. I saw it, but couldn't move. It was a direct hit in the middle of my chest. I had been speared! I dropped my ice cream and fell to my knees and butt simultaneously. The spear had hit me square in the middle of my chest bone, which is probably the only thing that saved me. But it hurt like hell. Ronald had no idea he could ever hit me. He was wide eyed and frozen in the tree like a mannequin. I don't remember how long it took me to get over that. But I survived.

Recollections

"Sandy the Pig"

Once we had a pig named Sandy. We got her after the hog raising fiasco. She was a pretty nice pig with a decent pig personality. We used to ride her around the pig lot because she didn't scream and run off like the rest of the pigs. We all got kind of attached to her. We would feed her well and rub her belly. But, all of a sudden she disappeared... vanished. Nobody had seen or heard from her in a week! Then, Dad noticed the top to the septic tank was off. You guessed it. Ole Sandy had done took a wrong step, one of the many hazards of farm life. We had to fish her out and burn her carcass immediately.

Recollections
"Peril of the Chickens"

One thing that was always in peril around the farm was the chickens. Any time we wanted to have a get-together or something, they were the handiest thing to grab and "whoop-up a good dinner" quickly. It was the funniest thing to me to watch them flop around after you had rung their heads off. Sometimes, they would do perfect somersaults over and over. I wondered how they could keep a balance with no heads! What might seem like cruelty to animals now was only a part of survival then. Everyone in the country back then lived the same way. When someone came over to visit and accidentally fell off the porch and broke an arm, there certainly were no lawsuits. The guest would more likely apologize for being so clumsy and that would be the end of it. But that was before lawyers and insurance agents were so thick. They are the only businesses I know of that create their own work. If they can cause a dispute or accident, they will. They actually do not like people that get along harmoniously. They pretend to be against each other, but actually they are business partners. One cannot survive without the other. No lawyer would sue a poor man with no insurance. Insurance agents point

Recollections

to lost insured lawsuits and tell their clients, "You need more insurance." If everyone was as poor as they were back then, lawyers could not survive.

Back to the chicken dinner. After the chicken was plucked, gutted and boiled for a while, it was ready to eat. What a feast we would have! You could always depend on Mother and Grandma Shipman.

Dennis A. Brown
"Grandma Shipman"

Once when Grandma Shipman was watching us for some reason, an old show called, "The Dance Party" was on. They were dancing and a song called, "Needle in a Hay Stack" came on. Grandma Shipman was sewing on a shirt button and she dropped her needle. She said, "Oh shit, I've dropped my needle." The song immediately replied, "Now you've lost your needle." We laughed at the coincidence for fifteen minutes, at least. Grandma Shipman was a big woman with giant breasts! But all of the sudden, she told us that it

Recollections

wasn't easy being such a big breasted woman. She raised the bottom of her boobs to prove it. She showed us the sores where her boobs rubbed her belly. Not a pleasant sight, and I don't know why she felt she had to share that with us, but you would have to know Grandma Shipman to understand. Grandma always claimed she had won a beauty contest where she grew up in Paragould, Arkansas. I used to always wonder if there were more than two in the contest, cause her beauty must have left her pretty quickly.

She never did let farts like we boys did. She just said, she "had a little gas." She said her doctor had told her not to hold it in because it wasn't healthy. Therefore, she farted no matter where she was or what she was doing with no excuses. She said she was just following the doctor's orders. "Good Hygiene." She would let them rip in the kitchen, at the store, in the car, or even at church during prayer! It didn't matter to her! She was going to remain healthy!

Grandma had bad knees and complained about them constantly. There wasn't a day that went by that she didn't say something about them. When the 4th of July would roll around each year, Dad would spring for some fireworks to be displayed in front of the other folks that had been invited over for chicken and other festivities. When night would fall, we would bring the chairs out from the kitchen and place them facing the cellar, 'cause that's where I would set the fireworks off from. Somehow, I was always the director of the show. I would give the announcements of what was fixing to go off next and what it was going to do. I was always careful not to shoot them towards the spectators. But one time in particular, I had a couple of what we called "spinners" that launched off simultaneously, both heading toward Grandma Shipman as if they were guided missiles! She saw them spinning toward her with their showering tail of sparklers. Before they could reach her, she had already begun to enact some defense maneuvers! She was on her feet and running! She had already left her chair, which was tipping over to fall, jumped over the septic tank lid, and did the limbo under the clothes line. She looked like a world-class obstacle course competitor! Of course, everyone was amazed at her agility and wondered if the spinners weren't what she had needed for a long time for therapy on those knees!

Recollections
"Grandpa Shipman"

Grandpa Shipman's name was Preston Shipman. Grandma called him "Press" for short. He was a fairly tall and slim man. He had worked in concrete most of his life. He and Grandma also argued continuously. But, it was mostly Grandma directing him on what he should do next. It was always, "Press, get this." or "Press, get that." or "Press, get the Kodak." Mostly it was that Press didn't do something right. I felt sorry for him in a way, but I guess it was a system they had learned to get along with.

Dennis A. Brown

They were mostly poor like the rest of us, but they got by somehow. Grandpa was a dreamer, and he dreamed specifically about the old cowboy days. I'm sure he felt he was one. They always had a horse or two and went to a few horse rides. He always dressed like a cowboy. But, mostly he just dreamed of being one.

I used to stay with them a lot. They lived in a small house in Dexter. They had a couch that would turn into a bed which I thought was the neatest thing I had ever seen! I loved sleeping on it. Grandpa would always go to bed early and Grandma would always stay up late and watch the late movie. I liked that, and usually it was a cowboy movie. She would lay her leg up by the window fan and talk continuously about what was going to happen next on the movie because she had usually seen it before.

You weren't allowed to move very much in bed 'cause it bothered her for some reason. She would always tell me to, "Be still! You're like a worm in hot ashes!" Then, after the movie, she would go to bed and snore like a hibernating bear! Then, early in the morning before daylight, Grandpa would get up, fix his breakfast and dinner, and then go off to work. The pattern remained the same.

In later years, Grandma died of cancer. It was a slow, miserable death. After her death,

Dennis A. Brown

Grandpa wrote a poem about her and put it in the local paper. He showed us an ability nobody knew he had. It was a fairly deep thinking, nostalgic poem about her and her passage into the after life. But her death somehow released a happier person in him which I felt had been contained by her dominance. He married again in a few years and lived several more happy years pretending he lived a hundred years ago.

His final days came when he was about eighty-two. He got into a log crosscut race at the local fair in Pocahontas, Arkansas. He and his partner won the race, but shortly after, Grandpa suffered a heart attack, which destroyed much of his heart. Back then, it wasn't feasible to operate on a man that old. They offered the option of staying on the machines or unhooking them. His children asked him for his direction and guidance as to what he wished for. He opted to be released. They held his hand and removed the machines and he quietly slipped away.

Dennis A. Brown

"Sonny and Donnie"

One thing I also remember is the card games my family used to play. They would get together and play a game called "High Nine." They would play it all the time. I remember it was mostly Uncle Sonny and Aunt Alice, who was my mother's younger sister, that used to come over and play. I would get on Dad's lap for hours watching them smoke cigarettes and play cards.

I had two uncles with two very different personalities and philosophies of life. One was Uncle Sonny and the other was Uncle Donnie,

Recollections

my mom's brother. Uncle Sonny was a hard working, hard driving man, good hearted on the inside but rough as a cob on the surface. He was always cussing, working, and suing somebody or being sued by somebody. It didn't matter who was into a fight, he was happy to be there. He always seemed upset about something.

Uncle Donnie, on the other hand, was laid back. He didn't seem to care if the sun shined or not. He drank a fifty-gallon keg of whiskey each year and seemed to enjoy everything there was about life. Uncle Sonny had my respect and Uncle Donnie had my admiration. Both of them were making it through this world in their own way.

Recollections
"The Motorcycle"

About this time, Ronald and I were at the motorcycle age. We had somehow talked Dad into buying us one. We went to Cape Girardeau and settled on what they called an Eighty Suzuki. It set us free again, but was another delicate partnership. Ronald had this particular game he seemed to enjoy on the motorcycle. Garry and Larry had noticed him coming down the road passing the driveway, turning around, and doing the same thing over and over. They finally asked him what he was up to and he told them he was playing a game.

Dennis A. Brown

They asked him what kind it was, and he said he was trying to get as close to the mail box as he could without hitting it. Trying to understand the end result of it all, they looked at each other, and simply walked away. Ronald continued on with his personal death-defying act.

We wore that motorcycle out. There was nothing better at that age than the ability to get almost anywhere you wanted to go... "Aahhhh, freedom." In the country, nobody ever checked for a license.

We rode that motorcycle so much that we wore the drive cogs off of it. One of the last things I remember about the Eighty Suzuki is

Recollections

that I had been riding it in the mud and the front fender kept getting plugged up with mud. So I devised a good plan to alleviate the situation. It had four bolts that held the fender on. I decided to take out two of them and raise the fender to the top two bolts. This seemed to work fine with just two bolts holding it until I was going down the road in front of the house one day in nothing but my short pants. I had her open to about 40 miles an hour when the fender rolled forward, hinging on just the two bolts which locked up the front wheel. I can still remember to this day rolling down the gravel road like it was in slow motion. I can still see my legs and arms going around and around and finally rolling to a stop in the ditch where the sewer drained. I had gravel cut wounds all over my body. When I came out of the ditch, I looked like a bleeding sewer monster. Ronald came running out as if to help me and ran past me and directly to the motorcycle to assess the damage. I struggled toward the house to look for help. Mother had seen what had happened and met me halfway and told me to go around back because "Mr. Brown" was here and she didn't want to upset him. I took several baths before the water became halfway clean looking. For a few months, I was scabbed over so bad that I could

Recollections

hardly move. But I finally worked out of it and was ready for the next part of my life.

And the next parts of my life were always hazardous. Dad was always tied up in work and believed that we should learn on our own, I guess. "Cause looking back, he really didn't watch us all that close. While we were threshing with the combine, he would let me crawl all over the thing. I mean I would crawl around the grain tank where there were several augers running, back around the engine where belts were turning and around the sides of the combine. I might even walk the wheels while they were turning. I guess he had pretty good confidence in my intelligence and balance. So, we kind of learned on our own to be careful around things.

The only time I was really a little scared is when we were moving dirt one day with an old tractor and dirt scoop. I had been watching the dirt pile into the dirt scoop, piling it up to the top and thought it would be pretty neat to get in there and walk up on the dirt while it piled up. I told Dad what I wanted to do, and as usual he said it was okay. When I got into the dirt scoop, the dirt started coming in a lot faster than I had anticipated. Next thing I know, I'm up at the top, holding onto a bar that helped brace the outside of the bucket, and when the bucket was full, the bar would swing to the back of the bucket. And when it did swing back, I was pinned to the back of the scoop. It stopped within an inch of crushing time. So there I was, flattened by the bar to the dirt. I couldn't holler 'cause it wouldn't do any good. So, I just looked to see if Dad might be watching. And he was. He was watching straight ahead. He finally goes to where he wanted to dump the dirt, the bar came up, and I jumped back up on the tractor. I never said a word of what had just happened.

Sometimes I wonder...times were so hard and there were so many kids, not just in our family, but also in many other families... What

Dennis A. Brown

if you did lose one or two?...There were still plenty to go around.

Recollections

"The Old Pickup"

I remember once, times were so hard that we were down to only a pickup truck. Only about three of us could get in the cab and the rest had to ride in the back. So we fixed it up. We put two lawn chairs in back against the back of the cab for two lucky people to set in. The rest had to set where they could. It was fairly embarrassing just riding through town that way. But, one day we ran into a problem. We had all loaded up and went to town. Going through town, Dad had run across a spot he wanted to parallel park in. So, he pulled up to back into it and a car pulled in right behind him so he couldn't back up. So there we were, a Mexican stand off. Dad wouldn't go on and the car wouldn't back up. Before long, several cars had piled up behind the first and one of them was a police car. Dad stuck to his guns. He wasn't about to budge. By this time, several people were watching, and those of us in the back of the truck were starting to get embarrassed. Still, Dad wouldn't budge. We started asking him to please pull away. This only made him more resolved to stay. The other cars started honking their horns, increasing the embarrassment. I laid down in the bed of the truck till Dad finally pulled

Recollections

away. When I got up, the police car had pulled up, and the policeman asked Dad what the problem was. Dad told him and the cop pulled away. Another part of my life...etched in my mind.

Dennis A. Brown

"King of the Throne"

Early in the mornings, Dad would always start his day off by setting in the blue cloth chair we had in the living room. He would get a cup of coffee, fire off a cigarette, set in the chair in his underwear and let out farts while watching the news. I would find him in this position many mornings. I could always tell when he had gotten up because his smoke would go from the front room, through the kitchen, up the stairs to our room and I would smell it. My young, pure lungs would not

Recollections

accept it and it would almost halt my breathing.

There wasn't much privacy in the house back then. I remember after Dad had his coffee, it was time for the king to take to the throne. The only problem was there were seven other people trying to get to school and work. He sometimes had to conduct his business with an audience coming in and out. I'll never forget once when he was on the throne, there were several of us boys in the little bathroom. He looked up and said, "Can't we find just a couple more to get in here?" But, we made it work out somehow.

Dennis A. Brown

"Morning Games"

There was always a little game that I and some of the others would play with Dad. Being young, it was hard to get up in the mornings. It was especially hard to get up when it was cold because there wasn't any heat upstairs. First, Dad would holler, "Boys, it's time to get up." in his bear voice. Next, he would repeat his message while flashing the upstairs light. Next came the command, "GET UP!" That's when I would drop my leg out of the covers and hit the floor a few times with my foot and make it sound like we were moving around. This would gain us a few more minutes. But on his last attempt when you heard his foot hit that first step coming upstairs, we were up and running.

Dennis A. Brown

"The Junk Hole"

Once, Dad had dug a big hole out back of the house and was burying junk in it. It was just left open, and when it got full, he was planning to cover it up. Well, it was a Sunday evening after a big rain that night. Mother and Dad had decided to get in some quality arguing time. Debra and I had decided to escape some of it and were playing in the water out back. Then, she dared me to jump in that big hole. Without thinking, I jumped. In mid air, I remembered what was there... too late. When I hit, my left heel landed on something sharp.

Recollections

Carefully walking out, I examined my heel. It was hanging open with blood gushing out. I showed it to Mother and Dad. That broke up the argument. Mother took off walking down the road and Dad held my heel together to stop the bleeding. Then we just taped it together to heal.

Dennis A. Brown

"The Auction"

There used to be quite a few people in the community. Therefore, we had quite a few people in our church at Frisco. We had many various social get togethers. But the one most prevalent in my mind is the time we had a box supper. We were there earlier than some. It was dark, and I was playing on the roof for some reason. Then, Edna and Welza Swinger pulled up. Hidden in the dark on the roof, I heard Edna tell Welza, "You be sure and buy this box 'cause I didn't fix very much." AH, HA! I had found the inside track! I was going to make old Welza pay top dollar for that. I scrambled off the roof and into the church to get into a good bidding position. They fired off the bidding and when it came to Edna's box, I commenced to bidding. Each time Welza would bid, I would hit it another lick till all of a sudden, Welza quit! Hung on $7, no one else would pay that much. It was hollered, "SOLD" and I looked at Dad. "I hope you got some money," he said. While I was embarrassed and gulping for air, Edna came over and said she would share it with me and we split the price. The moral of the story is... "The inside track is not always that good of a deal."

Dennis A. Brown

"Jackie and Rufus"

Around about 1964, blacks were integrated into our school system. The "white boys" weren't very nice to them. We weren't encouraged by anyone to be mean to them, but it seemed like the teachers would turn their heads when we were. It seemed like the system was trying to change, but it also seemed like some of the families of the old system weren't in agreement. But after getting to know them and not being afraid of them, we got along just fine. And many became good friends of mine.

Recollections

I remember Ronald, me and two black friends named Jackie and Rufus were chopping cotton for Hubert Swinger in front of the old home place. We would watch the clouds as usual and talk. Funny thing about the cotton patch...no one was better than the other out there. We were all equal. I remember Ronald's friend Jackie would talk about all the great things he was going to do. Although I was skeptical, his confidence in his speech could make you believe he could make it. And there was another tough hurdle. Jackie was mildly deformed. His left foot was deformed to the point of turning ninety degrees toward his right foot. He had what appeared to be the shape and size of an index finger protruding from his side. I noticed, but never asked what it was. But, the kid played basketball as hard and almost as good as anyone and never complained about his handicaps. He would tell us of all the great things he was going to do and I wondered how. It was bad enough to be a poor white boy in a cotton patch, but how could a poor black boy in 1969 ever dream of making it out of there? But, he did. Jackie became a professor and now helps others wanting to get out of the proverbial cotton patch make it.

It seems ironic to me now. If people saw us living now the way we lived then, the social service people may well have taken us away. However, things were different then, and it seemed like in our little world, everyone lived the same. So, this concludes my compressed thoughts of a boy raised on a small farm in Frisco, Missouri.

Dennis A. Brown
"The Family Tree"

My Grandpa Brown came to this part of the country from Illinois. He crossed the Mississippi River on a ferry and traveled by train surrounded mostly by swamp water to get to the spot. After building a house, he summoned Grandma to join him. He had to take a sled to Essex to pick her up because the water was up. After convincing her to get off the train and into the swamp, they began growing a family tree. What I have written is only a small portion of that tree. As for the family farm, Grandpa passed it on to Dad and another brother at a good price. I believed so that it could be kept in the family. Dad later bought the other brother out, which left us boys next in line to have it. But, later in life, Dad fell on hard times and had to sell the farm. Although it seemed a little manipulative, the farm fell into the wrong hands, the reasons of how and why would hurt too many people to explain. But I did find a great respect for people with money and power. It's sad to me, but they can make things swing their way. They can take the farm, but they can't steal the memories. And money is not the only power in the world. "There is still power in the truth" as spoken by a man who hardly wrote a word, but

Dennis A. Brown

changed the course of a world. After writing this, I somehow feel released. There is nothing stronger than the written word that comes from the heart.

Dennis A. Brown

About The Author

Dennis A. Brown was born to a large, lower income white American family. Although witty and entertaining from the very start of his life, he was soon to learn of the ups and downs of being raised on a small farm in Frisco, Missouri. Dennis is always intent on telling the truth no matter how it might hurt him. Blaming his bad memory as his reasoning for always needing to tell the truth, Dennis claims he couldn't keep up with his lies if he had to. After trying hard for many years to mimic or harness the "getting mad" emotion, Dennis finally gave it up and decided it wasn't in him. However, you will notice in his writings that he is very well acquainted with all the other natural emotions of the human life.

CPSIA information can be obtained
at www.ICGtesting.com
Printed in the USA
LVOW03s1800200717
541941LV00001B/1/P